The Unknown
GOD

Clinton Joseph Hall, Sr.

authorHOUSE®

AuthorHouse™
1663 Liberty Drive
Bloomington, IN 47403
www.authorhouse.com
Phone: 1-800-839-8640

Published by AuthorHouse   08/28/2012

ISBN: 978-1-4772-6614-4 (sc)
ISBN: 978-1-4772-6613-7 (e)

Library of Congress Control Number: 2012916131

Foreword

I began my Christian journey at the age of 11 as a Baptist and remained a Baptist for thirty years. When I first encountered Christ and the Holy Spirit, I was instantly healed and the Holy Spirit taught me how heaven will be when Christ returns.

I began my studies with Mr. Herbert W. Armstrong and the Worldwide Church of God until 1986 when he passed away. The church began to change their doctrine so I begin to research on my own. I found that Mr. Armstrong's ancestry went way back to Zephaniah. I found that he had an encounter with the Ukraine Brethren who could not speak English but could read the English Bible. Mr. Armstrong asked them if they wanted to join his church but they in return asked if he would like to join their church. So I found out that the Ukraine Brothers were Essenes. That was a group that goes back to 20 0 B.C. When he was young, King Herod, who was a common person, was grabbed up by one of the Essenes. Herod was beaten senseless by the Essene. Herod asked the Essene why he was being beaten. The Essene said be was beating Herod for future crimes that he would commit!

The Essenes had a spiritual knowledge of divine law. They lived a pure life and worshiped GOD and next to GOD they honored Moses. They healed the sick and raised the dead. They come in the spirit of Elijah and they were the forerunners of the Messiah. They did not believe in death. They believed that the body was the temple for the Holy Spirit. Roman soldiers use to get two horses, one facing one way, the other facing the other. They would tie the horses together and pull them (the Essenses) into two pieces. The Essenes would laugh at the Roman Soldiers and say that they were laughing because they were freeing them from the body. They traveled and in time ended up it England. Jeremiah, John the Baptist and Jesus Christ were Essenes.

The old Puritans were strictly Sunday keepers. They found out that Roger Williams was a Sabbath keeper, so they killed one of his friends, cut him up in quarters. So Roger Williams ran from the Puritans and came to the United States along with Peter Waldo and Steven Munford. They landed in New York and went to Rhode Islands because of the Puritans. Peter Waldo went to a Baptist church on Sunday but he kept the Sabbath with his wife at home. Then Ellen G. White took over changed the church to the Seven Day Adventists. They changed the doctrine more. This Is when Mr. Armstrong met them. So he left the Seven Day Adventists and started his own church. And the Seven Day Baptists started their own church. Mr. Armstrong moved to Oregon and he found out that there was more to keeping the Sabbath, the Holy Days needed to be kept as well. This was the end of the Sardis area.

Mr. Armstrong moved to Pasadena, California and started three universities, one in England affiliated with Oxford College, one in Pasadena, and one in Big Sandy, Texas. Royalty came to the University in Pasadena. One of the Queens stated that when she came to the University, she thought she was in Heaven.

Clinton Joseph Hall, Sr.

4

Preface

First, I am a 75 year old native of Greensboro, Georgia. Alcoholic beverages have been sold for as long as I can remember, whether it was legal or not. Cigarettes cause more deaths than alcoholic beverages, narcotics more than both put together. Yet cigarettes are permitted to be sold at anytime. If you want to vote on restricting the selling of anything, let it be cigarettes.

Secondly, if there is a vote to be had, I vote **YES** to the sale of alcoholic beverages being sold on Sundays. My reasoning is that some time ago ecclesiastical authority stated that you may search the Bible from Genesis to Revelation, and you cannot find one line or verse authorizing Sunday observance—that the Bible enforces the keeping holy the seventh-day Sabbath—and that the sole authority for Sunday observance is based on edicts of men.

The claim is that a succession of human ecclesiastical leaders has *replaced* the authority of Jesus Christ. This may surprise many religious people.

One of the arguments is that God's Commandments did not exist until the children of Israel reached Mt. Sinai. But Abraham *kept* God's commandments 430 years before his descendants reached Sinai. God is speaking. He is explaining *why* He made the great promises to Abraham. **SO ABRAHAM KEPT GOD'S SABBATH! THE SABBATH IS THE FOURTH COMMANDMENT.**

NOTE THOSE WORDS CAREFULLY!! It is the sign that IDENTIFIES to them who is their GOD! It is the sign by which we may KNOW that He is the LORD!! It IDENTIFIES GOD!

Clinton Joseph Hall, Sr.

5

Table Of Contents

Who Is God?...9

We Are Israel..11

Why Ten Tribes Became Lost! 11

Prophecy For Now 15

The Sabbath..21

The Unknown GOD 27

This Is My Prayer 49

To Benny Hinn And Reinhard Bonnke 71

Tower Of Babel...75

Epilogue 77

Appendixes..79

WHO IS GOD?

BUT DOESN'T EVERYBODY KNOW
WHO GOD IS?

ABSOLUTELY NOT! This whole world is deceived—so says your Bible (Rev. 12:9).

This world has a god—a false god—Satan the devil!
He pretends to be "an angel of light" (II Cor. 11:14).
He has his religious organizations. Not all are Buddhists, Shintoists, Taoists, Confucianists.

Many have appropriated the very name "Christian," whose ministers are actually Satan's ministers, says your Bible. "And no marvel, for Satan himself is transformed into an angel of light. Therefore it is no great thing if his ministers also be transformed as the ministers of righteousness" (II Cor., 11:14-15).

But do they actually call themselves the ministers of CHRIST? Read the verse just before the two just quoted—verse 13: "For such are false apostles, deceitful workers, transforming themselves into the apostles of Christ." Yes, Satan in the great counterfeiter.

He palms himself off as God. He is called, in your Bible, the god of this world (II Cor. 4:4). He palms off his ministers as the ministers of CHRIST—accusing the true ministers of Christ of being "false apostles" to divert suspicion from them!

Are there TWO KINDS of Christians? Read Galatians 3:28-29: "There is neither Jew nor Greek, there is neither bond nor free, there is neither male nor female: for ye are ALL ONE IN CHRIST JESUS. And if ye [ye Gentiles] be Christ's then are ye Abraham's seed, and heirs according to the promise."

So, since the Sabbath is BINDING TODAY on the Jewish part of God's Church, and there is no difference—we are all ONE in Christ—it is also binding on Gentiles!

WE ARE ISRAEL

But there is another answer to this argument: The people of the United States, the British Commonwealth nations, and the nations of Northwestern Europe are, in fact, the people of the TEN TRIBES of the HOUSE OF ISRAEL. The Jewish people are the House of JUDAH.

WHY are the Ten Tribes of the House of ISRAEL called "The Lost Ten Tribes"? AND WHY do our nations think they are Gentiles? WHY don't they know their true identity?

WHY TEN TRIBES BECAME LOST!

Here is a dumbfounding TRUTH, far stranger than fiction!

Here are FACTS, hidden for centuries, more intriguing than a mystery novel! WHY is the Sabbath called, disrespectfully, sneeringly, "the Jewish Sabbath"? Why does the world think all Israelites are Jews, and treat the Jews as ALL of the Israelites?

Here's an astonishing surprise to those who have believed that! The Jewish people are only a small minority of the Israelites, believe it or not! The very first place in the Bible where you'll find the name "Jew" or "Jew" is in II Kings 16:5-6—and believe it or not, there you'll find the Kingdom of ISRAEL, allied with Syria in a war against the JEWS!

Yes, there is it! ISRAEL at war against the Jews! Strange as it may seem, the children of Israel had become divided. They had become TWO DIFFERENT NATIONS! One was the Kingdom of ISRAEL. Its capital was not Jerusalem, but Samaria. The other was the Kingdom of JUDAH. Judah's capital was at Jerusalem. Now hear the strange story!

After the death of King Solomon, the people of the nation Israel rebelled against the high tax rate. The wise old Solomon lived in a state of luxury and splendor perhaps never equaled before or since. To pay for his great enterprises he simply kept raising the taxes.

The people demanded tax reform of King Rehoboam, son of Solomon. But he was young. He had young ideas. He surrounded himself with a "brain trust" of "whiz-kids" They, too, had young ideas. They counseled, "Tell the people you'll show them who's their master—tax them even higher than your father did." Rehoboam scorned the counsel of older, wiser heads. To him they were the reactionaries of his day.

The PEOPLE staged a gigantic mass rebellion. They rejected Rehoboam, and set up Jeroboam, who had been promoted to high position by King Solomon, as their king.

But the tribe of Judah dissented. Rehoboam was of their tribe, and they wanted to keep him as their king. So the tribe of Judah seceded from the nation of ISRAEL. They formed a separate kingdom, called the Kingdom of JUDAH. The tribe of Benjamin went with them. They became known as the Jews—NICKNAME FOR JUDAH.

Nowhere in the Bible are any of the Ten Tribes nations Israel called Jews. The tribes of Levites composed of the priesthood. They were leaders, best educated, and enjoyed incomes two or three times larger than the other tribes. Living off the tides with one swift stroke, Jeroboam demoted the Levites and set the lowest and most ignorant of the people to be priests. He could control them. The

Levites went back to the Kingdom of Judah and became known as Jews.

So immediately Jeroboam set up two great idols for his people to worship. He ordered the fall Festivals (including the annual Sabbaths) to be observed in the Eight month, at a place in the North of his choosing—instead of in the annual Sabbaths) to be observed in the Eight month, at a place in the North of is choosing—instead of in the seventh month, and at Jerusalem as GOD ordered I Kings 12:28-32). Through the rule of 19 kings and nine successive dynasties, the ten tribe house of ISRAEL continued in the basic twin sins of Jeroboam—idolatry and Sabbath-breaking. Several of the Kings added other evil and sinful practices.

But in 721-718 B.C., God caused the House of Israel to be invaded and conquered by the Kingdom of Assyria. These Israelites were removed from their farms and their cities, and taken to Assyria on the southern shores of the Caspian Sea as Slaves. But the House of Judah—the Jews—a separate and different nation, was not invaded until 604 B.C.

Two or three generations after the captivity of Israel, however, the Chaldeans rose to WORLD POWER, forming the first World-ruling Empire. Under Nebuchadnezzar the Chaldeans (Babylon) invaded JUDAH (604-585 B.C.).

The Assyrians later left their land, north of Babylon, and migrated northwest—through the lands that are now Georgia, the Ukraine, Poland, and into the land that is called Germany today. Today the descendants of those Assyrians are known to us as the GERMAN PEOPLE.

The people of ten-tribe Israel also migrated northwest. Though the Assyrians had taken Israel into captivity, the Israelites did not remain as slaves of the Assyrians in Europe. They continued on a little further—into Western Europe, the Scandinavian Peninsula, and the British Isles!

Now why did they come to be known as the "LOST TEN TRIBES"?

THEY HAD LOST THEIR NATINAL IDENTIFYING *SIGN*!

All of Israel's kings followed the practice of Sabbath breaking, a well as idolatry! As long as they remained in the LAND of Israel, and called themselves "The KINGDOM OF ISRAEL" their identity was known. But in Assyria they were no longer a nation with their own government and their own king. They were mere SLAVES. They took up with the language of the Assyrians as succeeding generations grew up. They LOST the Hebrew language. They lost all national identity.

After several generations, the tribe of Joseph divided into the two tribes of Ephraim and Manasseh which today are the British and American people.

The tribe of Reuben settled in the country that is France today. They had lost their national identify. But the French have the very characteristics of their ancestor, Reuben. Today, through a free booklet in the French language revealing this ancestry and national identity, thousands of French people are beginning to learn their own true identity.

The TEN TRIBES, known as the House of ISRAEL, lost their identifying tag—God's Sabbath. THAT IS WHY THEY LOST THEIR NATIONAL IDENTITY!

Prophecy for Now

PROPHECY FOR NOW

Note It! "For she did not know that I gave her corn and wine, and oil, and multiplied her silver and gold, which they prepared for Baal" (verse 8)

That pictures Britain and America TODAY! God has given us the unprecedented national WEALTH HE unconditionally promised Abraham's OBEDIENCE! But how have we used this wealth? In Baal-worship—the Day of Baal the sun-god, called SUNDAY—in Baal's Christmas, Easter, and other holidays—in the PAGANIZED so called "Christianity," much of which is the very antithesis of the true religion of JESUS CHRIST!

So, notice, verse 9, what God is going to DO about it! "Therefore will I return, and take away my corn in the time thereof, and my wine in the season thereof . . . ."—that is, the FAMINE already now beginning in its early years—prophesied by Joel, Ezekiel, by Christ, and in Revelation! Yes, this is a prophecy for NOW! FOR OUR PEOPLE! It is even NOW, as you read, beginning!

Continue! Notice what else God is NOW about to do to us: "I will also cause all here mirth to cease, HER feast days"—those of Baal—Christmas, New Year, Easter Lenten season, Halloween! They are NOT GOD's days! Continue: "her new moons and her Sabbaths . . ." (NOT GOD's, but those of Baalism, which our people call THEIR Sabbaths—the pagan SUNDAY!) (Verse 11)

God continues: "And I will punish her for the feast days of the Baals . . . . When she forgot me, says the Eternal" (verse 13, Revised Standards Version)

We are going to have such total DROUGHT and disease epidemics that it will take one third of our people and, unless our people as a nation wake up and repent of these SINS, we shall then be INVADED, and once more TAKEN CAPTIVE AS SLAVES. You may scoff. You may ignore. But NOT FOR LONG! In the near future it will STRIKE! You won't scoff then!

But what is the END of this particular prophecy of Hosea?

READ IT!

Therefore, behold, I will allure here [Israel], and bring her into the wilderness"—in slavery and captivity—and speak unto her heart . . . And it shall be at the day"—the time of the second coming of CHRIST!—"saith the Eternal, that thou shall call me Isaiah [Hebrew meaning MY HUSBAND]; and shall call me no more Baali. For I will take away the names of Baailim out of her mouth, and they shall no more be remembered by their Name. And in the day will I make a covenant for them" __ The NEW covenant! . . . and I will say to them which were NOT my people ["LOST" TEN TRIBES], Thou are my people; and they shall say, Thou are my GOD" (Hosea 2:14-23).

Probably you never understood the prophecy of Hosea before! It cannot be really understood unless you first understand the SABBATH COVENANT OF Exodus 31:12-171!

Ezekiel was given a message from God to the HOUSE OF ISRAEL (NOT THE House of Judah). Ezekiel was among the Jewish captive, after their captivity, more that hundred years after Israel's captivity. By that time the Assyrians had been defeated by the King of Babylon. They later left their land on the southern shores of the Caspian Sea and migrated northwest, finally settling in the land called Germany today.

The people of the House of Israel also migrated northwest across Europe. But they did not stop in Germany. They went on farther west and north—into Western Europe—France, Belgium, Holland, the Scandianian countries, and the British Isles—where they are to this day, except for the Tribe of Manasseh, which much later migrated to the United States.

CONTINUE THE PROPHECY

"And I will bring you from the people, and will gather you out of the countries wherein ye are scattered . . . with FURY POURED OUT, and I will bring you into the wilderness of the people [COMING EXODUS—Jer. 23:7-81, and there will I plead with you FACE TO FACE" (Ezek.20:34-35).

Notice it! This is the WORD speaking—CHRIST! HE will then be on earth again in Person! And then He is going to plead with our people FACE TO FACE. That will soon happen to YOU, and to YOUR LOVED ONES.

It's time to AWAKE to the imminence and the stark SERIOUSNESS of this!

Perhaps only one lone voice is WARNING YOU! But God used one lone voice to warn the world in Noah's day—one lone voice in Elijah's day—one lone voice in the day of John the Baptist, and after he was put in prison, in the Person of Christ Himself!

If you rely on the majority of sinning PEOPLE, you will suffer their penalties with them!

NOTICE HOW HE WILL PLEAD!

"Like as I pleaded with your fathers in the wilderness of the land of Eqypt, SO will I plead with YOU, saith the Lord ETERNAL . . . A I will purge out from among you the rebels, and them that transgress against me . . . and YE shall KNOW what I am the LORD" (verses 36-38)

How did He plead with them? He pleaded: "Hallow MY Sabbaths, instead of your fathers', so that you may KNOW that I am the LORD."

And how shall we KNOW that HE is the LORD? By His Sabbath SIGN!

Read verses 42-44 in your own Bible! He says our people, when they are no longer rebellious, who will then be keeping His Sabbath, shall remember their ways in which they were defiled, and shall LOATHE themselves for their Sabbath-breaking!

This is pretty strong teaching! It is the WORD OF GOD SPEAKING TO YOU!

Finally, to all of the self righteous ministers and followers of SUNDAY as the first day of the week, there is nothing HOLY ABOUT SUNDAY, THE SABBATH IS THE HOLY DAY! Mark 7:7-8.

The Sabbath

THE SABBATH

In the teaching of the Roman Catholic Church, according to the book, The Faith of Our Fathers, by Cardinal Gibbon, "You may read the Bible for Genesis to Revelation and you will not find a single line authorizing the sanctification of Sunday. The Scriptures enforce the religious observance of Saturday, a day which we never sanctified." This is an official publication of the Roman Catholic Church.

From the Catholic Doctrinal Catechism is this question:

"Have you any other way of providing that the Church [the Catholic Church] has power to institute the festivals of precept? Had she not such power, she should not have done that which all modern religionists agree with her, she would not have substituted the observance of Sunday the first day of the week for the observance of Saturday the seventh day, a change for which there is no Scriptural authority."

And also;
"When Protestants do profane work on Saturday, do they follow the Scripture as their only rule of faith? On the contrary, they have only the authority of tradition for this practice. In profaning Saturday they violate one of GOD's commandments which he has never abrogated."

From the Edict of the Council of Laodicea in 363 AD it this:

"Christians must not Judaize by resting on the Sabbath, but must work on that day, rather honoring the Lord's Day." And they called Sunday the Lord's Day. The Church pronounced any that honored Saturday and did not honor Sunday to be anathema from Christ. The Church at that time was, you could say, riding the back of the government and guiding it. The Church was superior to the government. Consequently, when the Church pronounced any to be anathema from Christ, they were arrested. At this time millions were persecuted and many tortured and many put to death.

In Theological Dictionary, a Methodist publication, by Charles Buck, is this: "Sabbath in the Hebrew language signifies rest and is the seventh day of the week, and it must be confessed that there is no law in the New Testament covering the first day [Sunday]."

From a Presbyterian publication, **Christians at Work** is this:

"Some have tried to build the observance of Sunday upon apostolic command, where as the apostles gave no command of the matter at all. The truth is, as soon as we appeal to the literal writing of the Bible, the Sabbatarians have the best of the argument."

In **A Catechism** by Isaac Williams, Doctor of Divinity of the Church of England is this: "And where are we told in scripture that we are to keep the first day at all. We are commanded to keep the seventh, but we are not where commanded to keep the first day. The reason why we keep the first day of the week instead of the seventh is for the same reason that we observe many other things, not because of the Bible but because the Church has changed it."

Matthew 12:38-40 says "The certain of the scribes and of the Pharisees and answered saying, "Master, we would see a sign from Thee." But He answered and said unto them, "An evil and adulterous generation seeketh after a sign; and there shall no sign be given to it but the sign of the prophet Jonas: For as Jonas was three days and three nights in the whale's belly; so shall the Son of man be three days and three nights in the heart of the earth." Tradition says that Jesus Christ was crucified and buried on Good Friday and rose from the dead very early on Easter Sunday. But how do you get three days and three nights between those days. That would be all night Friday night, all day Saturday, and all night Saturday night. That equals 1 day and 2 nights, not 3 days and 3 nights. This is the only sign Jesus gave that he is our Savior. If you deny that Jesus was in the tomb 3 days and 3 nights, then you deny the only sign he gave that identified him as Savior. Jesus Christ also said that after he was crucified and buried he would rise in three days. That can't be 2 days or 4 days. It must be 72 hours, not more, not less—3 days and 3 nights. Again, you can't fit 3 days and 3 nights between Good Friday and Easter Sunday. The answer is that Jesus was crucified on a Wednesday and the Sabbath day was drawing near (John 19:3). The Sabbath day in 31 AD was not a regular weekly Sabbath but was a "high day" (John 19:31), an annual Sabbath day that could occur on any day of the week. Therefore, Jesus was in the grave all night Wednesday, all day Thursday, all night Thursday, all day Friday, all night Friday, all day Saturday (3 days and 3 nights) and at the "end of the Sabbbath" (Matthew 28:1) he rose from the dead. Jesus Christ rose from the dead at the end of three days and three nights in the grave—Saturday evening, not Sunday morning. When the women came to the tomb early Sunday morning it was still dark and Jesus had already risen from the dead because the tomb was empty (John 20:1). The sun had not risen but Jesus had already risen from the grave. Many who keep Sunday as the Sabbath day say they do so because they believe Jesus Christ rose from the dead on Easter Sunday. He did not. He rose on a Saturday evening at the end of the Sabbath, at the end of 3 days and 3 nights in the grave.

It was Jesus custom to observe the Sabbath day. Luke 4:16 says "And He came to Nazareth, where He had been brought up: and, as his custom was, He went into the synagogue on the Sabbath day, and stood up for the read."

It was the custom of Paul, the apostle to the Gentiles, to preach to them every Sabbath day (Acts 17:2). He observed the Sabbath and taught them on the Sabbath. Paul also said in I Corinthians 11:1, "Be ye followers of me, even as I also am of Christ. Christ kept the Sabbath; Paul followed Christ in Keeping the Sabbath. Paul taught the Gentiles on the Sabbath.

In the book of Genesis God rested on the seventh day, and sanctified it. He created it for man when man was made. In the Ten Commandments it says to remember the Sabbath to keep it holy. But many will say the Ten Commandments and the law have been done away with. But I John 2:4 says "He that saith "I know Him," and keepeth not His commandments, is a liar, and the truth is not in him." Matthew 5:17-19 says "Think not that I have come to destroy the law, or the prophets: I have not come to destroy, but to fulfill. For verily I say unto you, till heaven and earth pass, one jot or one title shall in no wise pass from the law, till all be fulfilled. Whosoever therefore shall break one of these least commandments, and shall teach men so, he shall be called the least in the kingdom of heaven: but whosoever shall do and teach them, the same is called great in the kingdom of heaven."

What is sin? Jesus came to pay the penalty of sin (Romans 6:23). I John 3:4 says "Whoever committeth sin transgresses also the law: for sin is the transgression of the law," The Law is a spiritual law composed of Ten Commandments divided into the two great laws—love toward God and love toward neighbor. The first four show you how to love God, the last six show you how to love neighbor. And sin is violating that law in principle and spirit.

The Unknown GOD

THE UNKNOWN GOD

I would like to introduce you to an **UNKNOWN GOD**. When Paul was in Rome he talked to all of the brethren, they were not his brothers but they were all worshiping statues and all kinds of gods. Paul talked to them and stated that he saw that they really were religious because they were worshiping a statue called the Unknown God. That is what I would like to reintroduce you to, **THE UNKOWN GOD.**

We are going to take a trip in time and from there we will go to a place before time. It is more accurately to say a place that never existed. There it is not a place as we think of in terms of dimension. Where we are going is not in this creation. Because this place in non-dimensional, it does not meet the qualification of being a place that is no time. There is not space. No Down, No measurement. Where is this place? The place is GOD himself, GOD before Creation!

God is without dimension, therefore we cannot say that in GOD is a place as we move into GOD we make a discovery. We are Christ at GOD's very center and there we see Christ as he was before creation.

Christ did exist before creation. What was Christ, the creator of life, before creation and what did he do before he created. There are many things Christ did before creation. He was very active before creation. To go into GOD before creation means we journey into a time before time. A place when there was no place, no space, no measurement and no tick of the clock. These concepts were not in existence. To journey to the point before creation means we leave everything behind. There is no angel, no heavenly, no earth, no sky, not even nothingness, did not exit, no vast, no void, at that time before time there was not anything except GOD. There were not two things, GOD and nothingness. There was GOD and only

GOD. Not GOD plus nothingness, there was GOD and only GOD. Not plus nothingness, not GOD anything. GOD WAS ALL!

Nothingness, this non dimensional place which is GOD himself is the one and only place where we can safely say that all things that are there are real. This is a place where there is no shadows, no types, no replicas, no image, no picture of that which is real in GOD no unrealistic. Yes, GOD is a place that is before symbol. GOD is the only place where all is reality. This we must understand if we are to grasp Christ before creation. We live in a world before shadows, symbols, types, image and picture. For instance, we speak of gold but the gold we have here in the material realms is made of mass fill with protons, electrons and atoms in a place that give us no more than a picture of real gold. Real gold is Christ. Our goals here in this realm are mass is a suggestion of Christ. Also, the real son is Christ. Our son is a shadow of Christ. It is a picture of him. Before creation there existed in the father, in the son and in the Holy Spirit the real gold, real water, real food. There in GOD resided real water, food, light and life and there are no shadows, nor image, nor symbols, nor reflection. Before creation, gold was Christ. Water was Christ. Light was Christ. The sun was Christ. The moon was Christ. Then along came creation and creation was strewn with a picture of him. That moon up in the sky is not the true reality. That moon is a picture of Christ. Life was Christ. True life is Christ. All we have here in the fiscal creation is a shadow of life. Christ is life. Man body 71 percent water and 29 percent half of the 29 percent does not belong to him. Before creation began, Christ was everything and everything was Christ.

You and I and all things around us are shadows, pictures, image, replicas, and reflections of Christ. What was not in Christ was GOD before creation. What things were not present before creation? No laws, no legalism, no rules, regulations or observances. Such things did not and could not exist. Mark this, there was no bondage, there was no pray, there was fellowship though. Prayers did not come until after creation and until after the fall. Before that fellowship reigned, freedom ran free. Freedom was nothing less Christ himself. The only thing there was the

Father, the Son and the Holy Spirit. Nothing existed except the GOD HEAD all was reality. The only reality that ever existed there the trinity moved in a realm or absolute freedom which is natural imamate part of GOD. The GOD head was having a wonderful time but what were they doing? God head was fellow shipping the Father, Son and Holy Spirit. Yes the Father was the glory of the Son. The Son was glory of the Father. The Father adored the Son. The Son adored the Father. The Holy Spirit was the transport. So it was that one non day in the midst of this riches, this unobstructed immutable fellowship, the GOD head called a counsel. They counseled with one another and then agreed with their counsel. The GOD head decided that eyes other than the eyes of GOD should see the glory of the son. Such eyes that were not yet could see how glorious the SON is. The god head colluded together and decided to do something that one might say was a terrible gamble. Having made this awesome decision which included the gamble they worked out a plan, a purpose which guaranteed that the gamble would be no gamble at all. What the GOD had decided was immutable for the GOD head decided that there would be portions of the SON that would be chosen for some marvelous destiny. These portions of Christ were predestined, predetermined to a glorious destiny. The portion of Christ was marked out for the incredible. In that non time, it also strongly appeared that this blessed portion of Christ would one day be separated from Christ. But it only seems that way. It was a gamble that was not a gamble, a separation that was no separation at all. His plan was to resolve all these paradoxes. These portions through seemingly separated after space and time arrived had never been anywhere except in Christ. It simply is not possible to part the son from the son. All of GOD is in every part of GOD. Be it the Father or the Son or the Holy Spirit. All there is of the Father is in the Father. All there is of the Son is in the Son. A portion of GOD contains all of GOD.

So we have two enigmas, a gamble that is no gamble at all and part of the son, appointed some future destiny in space and time, remain in the son and containing all of the son portions of Christ—Chosen, Predestined, and Predetermined.

These portions of Christ awake their purpose somewhere out there in the future appearance of space and time continuum. But these glorious portions could only have their destiny fulfilled only if a creation appeared. Then the great drama of these marked off portions would begin. Absolutely no one knew anything about all of the activity. But that is because there was no one else you might say that the marked off predestined remained a mystery hidden exactly where it should be hidden in GOD. John 3:34. A mystery known only through GOD later, after creation, came into existence. We in creation would hear whispers of all these things but a very special moment in time all this activity remained only rumors before creation. And just what else might there be?

What has happened before creation? For one thing just before creation some things were present which were not GOD after the predestined ones were chosen and just before creation there appeared a book. This book listed the name of all of the names of the marked off ones. In this book the Lord wrote all of the predestined ones. Did this book have a name? Yes, the book was call the "BOOK OF LIFE." This is because it contained the name of all who would receive GOD own life in them. These are the very one who would receive eternal life. What is eternal life? Eternal life is a life form—GOD's own life. That form of life is the highest of all life form and is also called divine life. Christ is divine life. So it was that the GOD had wrote the name of those portions of Christ into the book of divine life in it was a record of all who would one day in time have divine life. It was a record of those who would have Christ in them. Out there in the distant future, it was also ordained that one day all those portions would come together. Or should we say come together again? In that coming together they would once more be utterly one, just as they were all originally one, part of Christ and one with Christ. In that future hour when all these portions would come together they would then become utterly one with one another and utterly one with Christ. Yet we must add this mysterious enigma those marked off portions of Christ were always past and future one with each other and always in Christ having written all these names in the book of the divine life. The Son closed the book and sealed it with the understanding that nothing could change GOD's election of those chosen ones. All would be there apart of him at the very end and into the forever more. Once that book closed nothing could prevent what GOD had purposed to accomplish with those portions. Those names were guaranteed forever to stay in Christ. No one could change that. So before creation there was GOD as all.

The Lord stepped forth onto the precipice upon which He would create. Would this be the moment when there would be other than GOD?

No, there was still more for Him to do before the actual act of creating. Several amazing things took place. Have you ever seen a little lamb? A lamb is really but a picture that tells us what Christ is like. Christ is the real Lamb.

Remember that terrible gamble (Which will turn out to be no gamble at all)? Once creation came into existence, God would allow all things to take their course, so things might not work out as God planned, hence, the gamble. But God did awesome things before creation to guarantee that all would work out as He planned, even though creation's inhabitants were free to plot their own destiny. And so it came to pass that before creation, all things were . . . well, it is a little hard to explain, so let us watch the drama.

Just before the act of creation, the Father slew His only Son. He slew the Lamb. The Father did this before creation. Never before had He slain His Son, nor would He ever again! Christ truly died before creation, before space-time. Christian, this is your Lord.

At the moment of the slaying of the Lamb, all those portions of Christ also died. What happened to Christ happened to them. His death was their death. Those marked-off portions of Christ were of Him, from Him, through Him, but most of all . . . in Him, when He died. And also when He rose!

This dying and rising happened before time, before dimension, before space, before creation.

Once, and only one, these predestined portions of Christ died with Christ and in Christ, never again to die.

When He rose, all those portions were still part of Him and therefore rose with Him and in Him. Hey rose but once, never before and never again.

Neither Christ nor the parts of Christ could ever die again. Death could not touch Him. Nor can Death ever again touch them!

So, you see, much did happen before creation. All these marvelous secret things took place before He created. What an incredible Christ. All this is Christ before creation! Nonetheless, as glorious as is all this, we have yet to come to the main point. Now we must face the inexplicable, just before creation.

Certainly, you and I must say that we were in that creation and we are part of that creation . . . or so we think. That you and I are in this creation, of this creation is not entirely correct. Of a truth we were not in this creation when it came into existence. As the pages of the history of this creation unfold, it strongly appears that you are of this creation; yet, as enigmatic as it is, you are not of the creation which Christ was just about to create.

No, you cannot be of this creation because you precede creation! After all, you were in Christ . . . before. When He visited here, He had a habit of speaking about before. For instance, He said, "Before Abraham was, I AM!" He said, "Those whom you gave me before." And in that moment, when He made those startling statements, you were in Him. You were there before Abraham. Why? Because you are, and were, in Christ. It is an oddity of this creation (the one Christ was about to create) that it has a clear, distinct beginning and an absolute end. Every atom, every molecule will be gone.

You will be present at the end. All things vanish. All! So, will you also vanish? If you vanish, then you truly are part of this creation. But if you do not vanish, then we can say you are not part of this creation. In the eyes of God, you are not involved in, or part of, this creation. Citizenship of this creation does not include you. Let us return to that moment just before Christ was about to call into existence creation. You were chosen in Christ and were part of Christ before He called creation into existence. (Part of you may be a great deal older than you realize. A part of you has been around a very long time. Even before time!) That is not all . . . there are the choosing, the slaying of that Lamb, the cross in Jerusalem, Christ's death, His resurrection, your redemption and, finally, the dissolving of this fallen creation. In mysteries beyond mysteries, all this was done away with before He created anything. To put it another way, Christ did away with creation before He created creation!

How is it possible for Him to destroy something He had not created? It is inexplicably true! Christ can do this. He does, you know! Your Lord finished all things before He created all things. Heb.4:3

How? The answer has to do with Christ's dwelling outside the passing of time. Remember that your Lord was doing all these acts in a realm where there is no space, no time, no up, no down, no mass, no measurement, no past, no present, no future. All that He did, He did in realms unseen, in that no-place called the eternal now! When space and time came into existence, the events that took place in the eternal now intersected with space-time. It is possible for the eternals to invade time and establish, in time, events that took place in the eternals. The events, thereby, happened in the realm of time, they seem real. Suddenly, what had happened in eternity was becoming real in time.

These events occurred before mass, before creation, before anything! That is, anything except God. And God made sure He had finished everything before He created anything! Dare we explore this enigma further?

Creating creation, giving man free will, and risking the Fall really did appear to be a staggering gamble on the Lord's part, but it was not so. Christ meant to accomplish everything first in eternity, to see that His will was carried out before He created.

Redemption was there before the Fall, before creation. Therefore, what appeared, in our eyes, to be a vast gamble had been taken care of before He said "Let there be . . . ." There were things done before creation that took care of crises that would happen after creation. When space-time did come along, the timeless intersected with time; the unloadable intersected with the locatable. The realities of what had happened before gradually became revealed during time. This is all inexplicable, or course. Things occurred on planes beyond our understanding. We really need to know only one thing: In realms of timelessness, your Lord resolved all the crises that would later occur in creation. To illustrate, you have seen that when your Lord was slain by His Father, those who were in Him died with Him, too. When Christ was slain, He took not only you, but also the creation (which had not yet been created), into death. Furthermore, the Fall (which had not yet occurred), and a Cross (which had not come), and a Satan (who did not yet exist), and Death (which had never been known), as well as the heavens and the earth (which were not yet created) all were taken into His being, and they all died with Him. He died! He went into a grave (a grave that was not yet). There, in the grave, He destroyed all those things.

Christ slew you, fallen man, the fall itself, and the sin of the world, death, the principalities, the powers, the law, and the entire world system when He was slain, before the foundations of the world. All of it was annihilated in that instant just before creation. Before creation, before all else, the Lamb took care of everything. The Lamb destroyed that which was not yet. A creation that had not been was placed in Him and then put to death, before He created it. Know this: The world you presently live in had imprinted on the back of its neck these words: CRUCIFIED BEFORE CREATED.

No wonder Christ is so assured about the final outcome: This creation was destroyed on the Cross before it was created. Before creation, not only was Christ slain by His Father, but so was everything else. But what of the resurrection?! This, too, took place before creation came into being. Resurrection, before? Yes! This is why Christ could declare, "I am resurrection."

Resurrection is Christ. Christ rose before anything was created out there in a spaceless, timeless, unseen, unknown and incomprehensible realm. What of all the things that were not Christ which also died in Him? There were not of Him, nor were they He Himself! Did they rise? No. In His pre-creation death, all other things were destroyed. They ceased to exist, forever. And, it happened before!

You must understand that this creation had already been slain and done away with. Amazing, is it not? Incomprehensible, is it not? We stand in awe of this incomparable Christ who is before creation. And part of you existed in that incomparable Christ before creation.

Still, we have not come to the main point. Now we come to yet greater revelation of this Christ who was before creation. WE are about to see the greater release of power that Christ ever unleashed. We now come to that moment when the triumphant resurrected Lord created.

That begs a question. If in that primordial age the Lord was all, then where did He place creation? There was no "out there" because Christ was all. Where, then, did Christ place creation? He could not place creation beside Him. There was no "beside" Him. After all, there was no place for even nothingness! There was no way to create creation without. Creation had to be created in Christ! (He is that great!) Creation, inside Him: That is where this creation is located, even today. Creation is inside Christ your Lord.

If you can see that creation in Christ, you can also see the resolution of much of the paradoxes, mysteries, and enigmas of our faith. After all, words like predestined, chosen, preordained, and foreknown could very easily raise a number of questions, especially when you add the words "free will". If we see the greatness of Christ before creation, the paradoxes vanish. This creation has a physical, geographic location; that is, creation is geographically locatable. Creation is located in Christ.

Today, right now, where is creation? In Christ; Christ envelops creation. Such is the greatness of your Lord!

Now we move a little further into this greatest of mind-boggling mysteries. Both the beginning and the end of creation are in Christ. There is a vast history in between these two statements: "In the beginning . . . ."(Genesis1:1) and "the first heaven and the first earth passed away"(Revelation21:1). One statement tells us about the beginning of creation, the other about the end of creation. Remember, if creation is in Christ, then Christ is at the beginning and the end simultaneously.

The dawn of creation starts at the beginning. On an on the story unfolds. He who is Alpha and Omega watches the drama. The drama reveals to us Enoch, Noah, Abraham, Moses, and David. Then the Cross and the tomb appear. There is Peter and there is Paul. As the drama continues to move forward, someone who looks a lot like you appears.

All this drama is in Him.

Christ was at the beginning of this drama, and Christ is at the end of this drama. Understand how this is possible. Christ envelops creation on all sides, making both ends of the drama happen at the same time because both are in Him.

Over here is the beginning; over there, is the end. Where is Christ? Is Christ stuck at the beginning? Is He stuck here, today? Is He at the end?

If He is stuck here, now, that would mean He would not know who made it to the end. That would rob Him of being the Omega, the end.

But Christ is stuck nowhere. He is in all places at all times because all places and all time are in Him. We might say that Christ need not ever move, because time is moving inside Him. Space-time began at the beginning and moves forward in Him. When space-time comes to the end of its existence, that final, last moment is also in him. He is there at the beginning; He is at the end. All is in Him.

This means the front and back, the top and bottom, the beginning and the end are in Christ. We cannot say of Christ that He is the Alpha and someday out there in the future He will become the Omega. Right now Christ is at the beginning and at the end of time, at the beginning and end of creation. Both, right now. There is where He is. There is where He always is. Right now your Lord is at the end. He is also at the beginning. There is where He is and where He always is.

Can we understand this? Of course not, we are shackled to three dimensions and captured in a seventy year time frame, in time, in space here. Outside space and time, Christ as the beginning and the end simultaneously, was not something that John Calvin understood. He was caught in space-time, too. Calvin had a God who was trapped in the present. Arminius had the same problem.

One of those men said "eternal security"; that is, once saved always saved! The other man said, "free will": that is, you can lose your salvation. Arminius said your name could be taken out of the Book of Life; Calvin said, "No it cannot."

Neither man grasped a revelation of Christ before creation, nor did they understand that creation is in Christ. Is there a way out of this dilemma? Can there be reconciliation? Yes, as we shall see.

See a Lord, free of space-time, who is at the beginning when the names of the redeemed are placed in the Book of Life. Christ is also at the end, and at the end there is the great throng of the redeemed, the gathering of the entire redeemed in one place. We know for sure that these saints described in Revelation 7 "made it"! They are all saved. On this point Calvin and Arminius agree! But Calvin would explain: "These were chosen before creation; none fell away. They are all here at the end, but were chosen at the beginning; and nothing can change that." Arminius, looking at the same throng, would declare: "Oh, no, God chose many more than these; but they exercised their free will, rejected the Lord, and/or some fell into grievous sin. Those who did not make it had their names taken out of the Book of Life."

It therefore came to pass that two separate views, one called Calvinism, the other Arminianism, arose! Neither fully grasped "in." But we need not look down on these two men; we do not understand "in" either. There needs to be no difficulty here. As we pass through time, from the creation to the end, man can, and does, exercise free will. He does so all throughout his journey, total free will. God does not interfere however, a sovereign Christ preordained us, created creation, destroyed creation, and knows the names of everyone in that great throng of the redeemed. He did the choosing and the predestining at the beginning.

Predestination and free will, how so? Is that not impossible? Not if you see that creation is in Christ and that Christ is at the beginning, where He always is, and Christ is at the end, where He always is.

May I now present to you the free will of man and the security of the believer, reconciled? Be advised, however, this was not written to discuss Calvinism and Arminianism. This is to reveal to you the greatness of Christ before creation and the greatness of Christ with creation in Him.

See free will and then see the result of that free will, at the end. The redeemed were chosen at the beginning, based on the fact that they had already been seen at the end. In that glorious moment at the end—where Christ always is—your Lord sees the redeemed ones and He moves backward through time until he comes to the beginning, where He always is. There He writes the names of the redeemed in the Book of Life based on those who made it to the end, based on the names of those who are in the great throng of the redeemed. Can He do that? Yes, because He is at the beginning and at the end, where He always is.

Let us see all this through the eyes of Christ. Christ says, "I know they made it and will be there at the end because I am at the end, where I always am, and I saw them there, so I place those names in the Book of Life. I did so before the beginning, where I am, where I always am." There, before the beginning, where Christ is, where he always is, He opens the Book of Life. He writes in the names of all those redeemed ones who were at the end. You know, those people whom Calvin and Arminius both agree are "the ones who made it." This should make both Calvinists and Armenians happy!

Are you wondering how it will all turn out at the end, who will be saved to the very end?

Let us do what Christ did. He went to the end where He is, where He always is, and while He was moving from the beginning to the end, He passed all places and all times, where He is, where He always is. He passed through the space-time continuum in all places, for He is there, no matter where "there" is.

Christ also came to you in your time, where He is, where He always is. He said, "Look! One of the ones who is in Me, who was in Me at the beginning and was in Me before the beginning, where I am, where I always am." So Christ went back to the beginning where He is, where He always is, and He opened the Book of Life to see if your name was written there. Lo and behold, there was your name, where it always is. Your name was in the Book of Life because you were at the end, where you are, where you always are.

Christ looked inside Himself and saw you, in Him, where you are, where you always are. Then Christ did a double check on you.

He came at last to the very end, where He is, where He always is, and, lo and behold, He saw you yet again. He saw you there in the great throng of the redeemed, singing "Thou are worthy, Thou art worthy."

He is always there. And you are always in Him. Why are you there? Because you are in Him before, at the beginning, and at the end. NO matter where you are, you are always in Him!

Having seen you in the great gathering of the redeemed, was He surprised? Did He call out, "Oh, you made it! You made it to the end. Oh that is wonderful!" Not likely! Perhaps this is what He did: Perhaps He said, "I am now going to choose, select, and predestine you. I will return to that time before time, before creation, before all things, where I always am, and there I will decide that you will be saved."

(He can do that, you know)

Then He went to the place where you were when you were calling on Him. That was easy! After all, he found you at the end, and He saw your name in the Book of Life before the beginning. At that "non-time" He elected you, chose you, justified you, sanctified you and glorified you.

See your dimensionless Lord, with creation in Him! Any yet, as glorious as all this is, there is a point more glorious still that is yet to be seen.

You definitely are one of those who "made it" to the end. But can we be certain of that? Let's put space-time in reverse, and see.
It is possible that we could say you were predestined at the end?
Perhaps your name was placed in the Book of Life at the end, and then the Book of Life was taken to "before the beginning!"

It does not matter where, when, or how! It is only that He did it. We will never fully understand the "how" until we escape the tyranny of space-time.

No matter where He is, at the beginning, middle or end, He is where He always is, and you are also there; you are always there.

Some Lord, is He not?!

Again, I must say to you, this is not the main point.

In the meantime, you have a low view of yourself? Then look at you, there in Christ before creation and there in that throng. In both places, you are so beautiful, pure and holy. You glow! In fact, because you were part of Christ in the beginning, and in Him you made it to the end, you are forever pure, honored, holy and indescribably flawless. Perfect and beautiful!

That is what you always are because you always are in Christ.

Further, you are all of that in both directions ← →in eternity past, in the present, and in eternity future!

There are some things you have a right to; there are some things you have no right to. You have no right to a basement-eye view of yourself. Somewhere out there in the mysteries of the eternal, where space and time just do not count, you are of the purest holiness. You share the holiness of God. Even today, you cannot be indicted. On this very day, you are blameless. No blame, no indictment, and absolutely no condemnation. You could be quite concerned about this as long as your thoughts are chained to this earth; but not in the realm where the clock does not tick, where past and future do not exist. Where you, being chosen in Christ before the foundation of the earth, and you, standing in the great throng of the redeemed, have both become one, you are as beautiful as the glorified Christ—because you are of Him and lost within Him."

Down here on earth, none of us look very impressive. But out there where the end is already over with, the sons and daughters of God, of whom you are one, look glorious! IF you could take flight from this fallen creation, if you could take flight from all space and time, and see what you already are—and what you have always been and what you will always be—you would be very impressed.

The Christ who is before creation, is He not becoming more glorious to you? Is He not ineffable, immutable in His glory? What Christ we have!

But again, this is not my main point.

Ever more glorious things await us.

Christ, somewhere in the eternals, cried out as did Adam, later in space-time, "I have no counterpart!" In that moment we see revealed Christ's purpose—His purpose for creating, His eternal purpose! His purpose in creating is to become one with His chosen Bride, His chosen, His predestined Bride.

What is her content? She is made up of all those marked-off portions of Christ, predestined to some great, glorious purpose. When those parts of Christ come together at the end, there is a moment when there emerges out of that throng Christ's own Bride, bone of His bone, spirit of His Spirit! There, out beyond the end, Christ becomes one with her. She is, in that moment of utter oneness, spirit of His Spirit, life of His Life. At last, out there beyond all time, there is finally, fully seen, the scene of all scenes, the moment of all moments. Paul speaks of it in that mysterious passage in I Corinthians 14:25. In that moment of union, Christ and His Bride will dissolve into the Father. Then He, who was once the All, becomes the All in All, oneness with God, the final, ultimate state, the purpose beyond all other purposes.

Wonderful, is He not!

All this is who your Lord is, Christ before creation, Christ beyond creation.

Dare to behold this matchless Christ before, during, outside of, at the end and beyond the end. This is your awesome glorious Lord.

Back when the Godhead counseled together, the Godhead decided that Christ would have a beautiful Bride. A Bride to match Christ. Can we possibly fathom how beautiful that girl must be? A woman or glorious as the Christ of the cosmos. I Corinthians 1:15-20

He is in her. She is in him. He is in the Father. The Father is in Christ. Ultimately, they all become indistinguishable, Christ, one with His chosen ones, one with you, one with us all. We are as much one with Christ as the Father is One with Christ! John 17

You are part of not only where He is, but you are part of what He is. Part of you is His very content.

You belong, and always have belonged, where He is.

But still, that is not the point!

The old creation, gone. Christ and His Bride, one.

The situation beyond the end of the creation is quite similar to the way things were before creation, when He was the All. Out there He is not the all; He is the All in All. Those portions of Christ who were at the beginning are also beyond the end. They are together, both before and after. Nor is it to be forgotten that they are in oneness in the middle, also.

Always one.

Before creation, dear honored one, you were in Him. Then time came along. You were still in Him. While He was dying as the Lamb (Revelation 13:8), you were in Him. When the Fall took place, you were in Him. You have been in Him ever since.

Out there, somewhere, when Christ allows this creation to dissolve (yet it has, of course, already dissolved), you will still be in Him. And remember, there will be no second creation to replace the old creation, but there will be the new creation revealed. The new creation is not made up of things created. The new creation is all that is left after the old creation disappears. This new creation is made up of things that are uncreated.

Christ, and you precede and survive the dissolutions of fallen creation.

Today you belong to the new creation. After the end, you will still be part of the new creation, which is made up of things uncreated. Also, behold, this new creation is older than the old creation. The new creation preceded the old creation and continues after the old creation. Is that possible?

Jesus Christ is before creation and after creation. Furthermore, Christ and all the parts of Christ are the content of the new creation.

You are the content of that new creation! Even that is not quite enough. More specifically, that part of you which was before is not created. That is, the best part of you is not a creation. Your body is a thing created. It ends when the old creation ends and it then completely replaced by a translated body. Your soul is everlasting, but not eternal. Your soul has a beginning, but no end ($\rightarrow$ everlasting),

What of your spirit $\rightarrow$ $\leftarrow$ eternal)!

As we have seen, your spirit is not of the physical realm. Your spirit is from the other realm. It appears that the believer's spirit is not even in this realm or of this realm. Your spirit belongs to the invisible realm. That means two-thirds of you is in this realm, and one-third of you is in the invisible realm!

Let us look at the "one-third" part of you!

Christ has placed Himself in you, in that one-third of you. Your spirit and His Spirit have become one . . . indistinguishably one. Not a blend, but one.

Part of your spirit has Christ in it. The two are one
(I Corinthian 6:17). Because Christ is not created, there is an aspect
of you that is also not of this creation. This "part" of you is life. It
is referred to as Eternal Life. That life is Christ! When you believe
on Christ, two things happened to you. First, your spirit was raised
from the dead. Second, Christ made His Spirit one with your spirit.
So, at the very least, a portion of you belongs with the eternals.

After the end of all things, Christ will be so much a part of your
spirit that your spirit and His spirit will be indistinguishably one.
You will have a translated body, a body permeated by Christ. You
will have a soul transformed and permeated by Christ.

That is you beyond the end. That will also be the state of all
believers. So it will be that Christ will have become all that is in
all.

You have caught a glimpse of how great and glorious is Christ
before creation. Now you have a glimpse of how glorious is Christ
after creation ends.

But up until now everything that has been said is but a background
to introduce you to the main point.

Let us discover . . . . the point!

Your name is written in a book that records the names of those who
have His content.

Is this not an incredible Christ, a Christ far beyond all we ever
dreamed?

But that is not the point . . . .

There is a point greater that all that has been said until now. Let us
see again just what Christ did before creation. In so doing, see your
glorious Lord, glorious things done by a glorious Lord. Consider
the greatness of this Christ, the Christ before. Never forget, the

Christ of the thirty-three years is also the Christ of the cosmos, the eternal Christ. The Christ who created such a vast physical universe that man has yet to find its end. This is your Lord!

It is the Father's desire that you know this Christ. He destroyed and then He created. He created and then He destroyed.

This Christ, the Christ before, is the Christ the Father determined would be first in all things. This Christ is now the enthroned Christ. It is by the might and power of this Christ that all creation is held together. This Christ will also one day wipe creation all away. This Christ chose you before the foundation of the world. This Christ chose you before the foundation of the world. This Christ loved you before the foundation of the world. This Christ died for you before the foundation of the world. This Christ makes love to you every day. This Christ will bring in all the portions of Himself together. Out of us will this Christ call forth His Bride. This Christ is going to marry that beautiful girl!

What a glorious Lord!

Today this Christ is the very content of the church. The "ekklisia" is the enlargement of this Christ. This Christ loves her, passionately, of whom you are a part.

This Christ is the first. This Christ sits enthroned. This Christ was and is . . . the real Lamb. This Christ is reality—the reality of all the shadows, types, symbols, images and pictures found so abundantly in creation. All creation is but a picture of this Christ.

Yet all that has been said of Christ pales in the glory of the main point. The main point is incomprehensible. It is this final, supreme fact which drove men like Paul!

This glorious Lord who created all things, this glorious Lord with all creation in Him, this Lord who finished all things before He created all things, this Lord who chose you in Himself before the foundation of the world, this Lord who wrote your name in the Book of Life, either before the beginning or at the end or somewhere in between, and who turned the greatest of all gambles into no gamble at all, this Christ who was slain before creation, this Christ who is the glory of the Father, this Christ who is the ALL, who will be, and is, the All who is in All, this Christ who is the beginning and the end, this Christ who is free of, above and beyond and outside of, all space, time, and even eternity . . . . this Christ has a point to make, message to bring to you.

The point, the main point, the incomparable point, the point above all points, a point you must spend the rest of your life considering and laying hold of is . . .

This Christ Lives in You!!

It was God's will to make known what are the riches of the glory of the mystery, and to make known to you that this Christ—this Christ, dwells in you!!

Christ in you: the Mystery! This awesome, endless, immense Christ is living in you right now.

He lives in you!

Upon what is the church built? The church is built on a revelation of the Lord, this Christ.

The ultimate end of this revelation of Christ is that this Christ lives in you!

This is My Prayer

THIS IS MY PRAYER

Heavenly father, in the name of Jesus Christ of Nazareth I come to your throne, to let you know that I love you with a perfect love that comes from the Father, Son, and the Holy Spirit. I come to let your holy Son on your right hand know that I love him with a perfect love that comes from the Father, Son and the Holy Spirit. I want the Holy Spirit to know that I love Him with a perfect love that comes from the Father, Son and the Holy Spirit. I want to thank you Holy Father for sending your precious Son, your only begotten Son come down to shed his precious blood and give us his precious life. He tore down the wall of tension between me and you. He revealed you to me, taught me of you, brought a message from you to me that I could be born into the God family with my heavenly Father's holy seed, heavenly Father's holy DNA sealed it with my heavenly Father's Holy Spirit for the day of redemption. Made out of my heavenly husband Christ Jesus' flesh and bone, heart, mind, soul, spirit, brain, doorway into his brain, uncreated not made with hands, hid in Christ Jesus with God the Father, except the piece that broke off for new Jerusalem, the lamb's wife, I thank you Christ Jesus for sending the comforter down like you said you were going to do, that precious, precious Holy Spirit that wrapped his Holy Spirit around my spirit until I become Holy Spirit. He wrapped my inner most being, my heart, my soul, my conscious my doorway to my brain, my mind, my thought, my will, wrapped it up with his Holy Spirit so Satan's nature and no human flesh has any pull on me. But when Satan fires his fiery darts at me he is only building spiritual muscles in me, just like a dumb bell in a gym. Because I'm in a comfort zone, Satan you can't see me, I'm in Christ Jesus and Christ Jesus is in me. I want to thank you holy Father for being my father I want to thank you holy Christ Jesus for being my lord, master, savior of my life. I want to thank you Holy Spirit for being my comfort, my guide, my protector, my teacher, my everything, teaching me about the God family, God the Father, God the Son and God the Holy Spirit, teaching me about my lord and master savior of my life, Christ Jesus. I wonder how precious how glorious how magnificent you really are, what you had to give up for man's sins. He had to pull off all this glory that he had with the father way before eternity. He stripped himself of all this glory in heaven. God the Father wrapped himself around him and the Holy Spirit carefully lowered him a little lower than an angel so he could become man and feel man's infirmity, feel how weak and frail man really is. Man could die for his sin or salvation. That's why Christ Jesus had to shed his precious blood and give us his precious life in order to tear down the partition wall between God the Father and man. This awesome God, this almighty God, this precious God, this Holy God, this righteous God, learned obedience by the things he suffered but after he suffered, he perfected, after he perfected perfection, he perfected perfectness and became the author of eternal perfect salvation for those who loved him and obeyed him and he became the author and captain of their salvation, bringing many sons to glory. That's why he is not ashamed to call us brethren.

God the Father could feel man's infirmity, he knows how man really feels but couldn't die for man's salvation. That's why Christ Jesus had to shed his precious blood to give us his precious life and that's why he had to become captain of our salvation, to make it sure by bringing many sons to glory. That's why he's not ashamed to call us brethren. This holy God, this righteous God, this almighty God, this precious God had to lower himself just to step down into eternity, so heavenly Father, in the name of Jesus Christ of Nazareth, I come to your throne. Let your Son come on down and set up your kingdom and start your government ruling back on earth as it is in heaven. Put away Satan for a thousand years, loosen him a spell so that the scripture can be fulfilled then put him away forever and ever. Burn up everything he ever touched, he ever made and let him watch it until the last piece is burned up then let him hear that sucking sound. I'm not asking for me only but the one who has the first fruit of the spirit that's moaning and groaning until now. I'm even asking for the whole heaven and universe and everything in it that's moaning and groaning until now and in chalk and the decay of confusion and illusion in bondage until now, waiting on the redemption of the son of God waiting on the

holy pieces marked off in Christ Jesus, the holy pieces with names
on them seen and unseen, visible and invisible, your precious
sons and daughters, can be about our Fathers business to let your
precious Son come on down and accept your kingdom and start
your governmental rules back on earth as it is in heaven. Put
away Satan for good this time and burn up everything imaginable.
Everything Satan ever made, let him watch it till the last piece
is burned up then let him hear that sucking sound, then Michael
will drive him to the edge of the pit then Satan, you will bow your
knee, and your tongue will confess that my Lord, my savior of
my life, Christ Jesus, is Lord, the sovereign God, the name above
ALL names. That's the last thing that will come out your raggedy,
stinking mouth, Satan. Then you will hear that sucking sound for
the last time. Then God's holy angels and the holy pieces that are
marked off in Christ Jesus, we can be about our Father's business.
First we have to purify the earth one more time because Satan is
just like a skunk. He is going to leave a skunked smell in the earth.
Then we will purify the earth one more time. Then GOD the Father
will come down to the earth and bring New Jerusalem down. New
Jerusalem, God the Father, God the Son, God the Holy Spirit
become one as we are one. Look at your Son on your right hand
and watch his beauty. He is going to be broke up into billions and
billions of pieces, the holy pieces with names on them, seen and
unseen. Your precious sons and daughters and your holy angels, we
can really be about our Father's business. We are going to shake
not only the heaven and earth but also the universe. Everything
not solid will be folded up and blown away. Everything not solid
will be built on a new heaven and new universe. The sons of God
will do what Satan's old evil angels refused to do. We are going to
take charge of the entire universe, create new plants, moon, sun,
and stars, glorify, purify, magnify and look back on what we have
done and look forward to what we are going to do because God the
Father says whatever be marvelous in your eyes will be marvelous
in his eyes.

Then God the Son will deliver the kingdom back to God the Father
so he can be all in all. Then God the Father will fill up the whole
heaven and universe through his sons and daughters. Billions and

billions of his sons and daughters turn the hold universe into a holy temple for our heavenly Father and Christ Jesus to dwell in, so he can watch our beauty while we are being about our Father's business, forever and ever and after that.

Speak that day. Glory, hallelujah! Glory, hallelujah! Glory, hallelujah! Glory, halleluiah! Glory, hallelujah! Amen. Amen and amen. "Our Father in heaven, hallowed be your name, your kingdom come, your will be done, on earth as it is in heaven. Give us this day our daily bread. And forgive us our debts, as we forgive our debtors. And do not lead us into temptation, but deliver us from the evil one: For thine is the kingdom, and the power, and the glory, forever. Amen." Matt 6:10-13. Thank you, Jesus. Father, I come to ask you to forgive me for all my sins, wash me down with the blood of the lamb so that you can't see my sin anymore. I repent of all my sins God. I'm sorry for all my sins Lord Christ. I repent of all my sins so that all my sins can go in the land of forgetfulness Father. I ask you to keep beating back Satan and keep him confined to the earth till Christ come with his holy angels to put him away for a thousand years. Loosen his spell so the scripture can be fulfilled and put him away forever and ever. Burn up everything that is imitation. Burn up everything he ever made and let him watch it until the last piece is burned, then let him hear that sucking sound. Heavenly Father I come to your throne in the name of Jesus Christ of Nazareth. I come to your throne and I come to thank you that Christ was sacrificed for all my sins so he could shed his precious blood and gave up his precious life for all of my sins. He tore down the partition wall between me and You. He revealed you to me, taught me of you, brought a message of you to me that I could be born into the God family with my heavenly Father's holy seed, heavenly Father's holy DNA and sealed it with my heavenly Father's Holy Spirit for the day of redemption. You put me on the robe of righteousness. You begot me with your holy divine seed, your holy, divine DNA. You sealed it with your holy divine DNA for the day of redemption. You loved me before I loved you, so I can say like your precious son Christ Jesus said nearly two thousand years ago, "Oh righteous Father the world doesn't know you, but I know you", because your precious

Son Christ Jesus revealed you to me and he taught me of you. So I can say like your precious son Christ Jesus said "Oh righteous Father the world doesn't know you but I know you because you loved me before you laid the foundation of the world." Oh righteous Father, you gave me back to Christ Jesus so he could mold and shape me in his image. Christ forgave all of my sins so he could mold up and shape us in our heavenly Father's character, his divine nature, his divine attributes and charity, the perfect love of God, everything in Galatians 5:22-23. Spiritual gladness, the first love I once had with Christ Jesus' living faith, your joy, your mercy and your truth, let this mind be in me that was also in Christ Jesus. Father I come to worship you in spirit and in truth because you are holy you are worthy to be praised. You are divine, you are precious, you are the sum of all beauty, glory, mercy and truth and love, perfect love of God of longsuffering, you are holy, you are worthy to be praised. You let me sit in high places in Christ Jesus. You let my name go out into all the cosmos, the atmosphere, the human sphere, you let me hang out with the holy angels, you let me hide deep, deep, deep in Christ Jesus so unfamiliar spirits can't spy me out, they can't attract me they can't trace me, it's almost impossible for them to find me because I'm in Christ Jesus and Christ Jesus is in me. When Christ Jesus died on the cross, hung on a tree, a stake, I died. When he was put in the heart of the earth, I was put in the heart of the earth, I was baptized in a watery grave, I was baptized with John's baptism. I repented but way, way down the line in 1979, I was baptized with the Holy Spirit in the name of the Father, in the name of the Son and the Holy Spirit, through the laying on the hands, I received the Holy Spirit. Then the Lord's commandment took occasion and came along and slew me and I died, but when Christ Jesus was resurrected, I was resurrected and became a new creature, a new creation, a new species. I'm in Christ Jesus and Christ Jesus is in me. I have his heart, mind, soul, spirit, doorway to his brain, one third of my life and one third eternal being are marked off in Christ Jesus, the uncreated, not made with hands. I am hidden in Christ Jesus with God the Father right in the center of Christ Jesus, except the piece that broke off for New Jerusalem, the lamb's wife so I'm in Christ Jesus and

Christ Jesus is in me, except the piece that broke off for New Jerusalem, a pillar or a column.

To all you false prophets and false churches, you say, "I sit as a Queen. I am not a widower. I have made lies and falsehood my covering. I have made a covenant with death and hell." But Christ Jesus says your punishment will happen to you in one day and one hour. The lies you cover yourself with will be blown away. All of your nakedness will show. You will become widowed in one day. The covenant that you made with death and hell will be annulled. Death and Hell with you both will be vomited up, just like Satan the devil. He will not be buried with his comrades, because the earth will not accept him. His comrades will rejoice in seeing him coming but the earth will not accept him either. How are you fallen, Old Lucifer, sun of the morning. How have you become as weak as we are, down in the pit with maggots under you and worms under your wings. You who shook the nations, would not open the prisoners doors, unbalance scales, feed the poor rotten meet and molded bread. You struck God's saints with a continuous stroke. But the earth is not going to accept you. Because you said, (Leviathan) "This is my river. I own this river. When I tried to take over God's throne, Christ Jesus burned me up with that white fire, kicked me out of heaven and when I came to myself, I was bouncing up off of the earth. The earth was sticking out of the water. The earth was covered with water. I was burned up so bad I had to grow scales over my whole body just to survive. I was burned up so bad all of my beautiful hair was burned off. I was walking on a silver cane. Some of my hair now is trying to grow back. It grows back in bunches. So when I covered my entire body with scales I learned how to travel underground. I cut me a river. I made myself a river, put my name on that river. That is how I got into the Garden of Eden and told Eden the first lie. So I own this river, you can't harpoon me. You can't destroy me. My scale is too thick. They are too close together and wind can't even get to it. So you can't destroy me."

But Christ Jesus says to Old Lucifer!, "When I first created you, you were perfect in all of your ways. Until iniquity was found in you, the spirit of jealously of man was found in you. I created all kind of musical instruments in you. I created pianos, harps, horns, pipes, organs, drums, and tambourines. You were a walking machine. But I also created a mechanism in you what I will use to destroy you within. The mechanism in you will explode inside of you. Old Lucifer, Sun of the Morning, in the twinkle of an eye you will be changed from spirit to matter. All of your wicked angels in high places above Mars in the snowy mountains will be pulled downed and stick to the old scales that you are so proud of. The illegal demons on earth will stick to your scales also." Angels do not like the earth or hell because they hate man. Hell was made for angels not man. Christ, when he died on the cross, bought the deed of man back in the golden casket, took the key of death and hell and fastened you up in hell. Christ says he will then put a hook in your mouth and pull you out of that river that you are so proud of into an open field and let you know who owns that river. Those illegal demons and evil angels that are stuck to your scale will be turned into matter. He will round up all of the meat eating animals and call down the foul of the air, the buzzards of the air and the crows that multiply real fast now. They will come down to the great supper. They will eat off of you Satan and your illegal demons and your evil angels for breakfast, lunch, brunch and dinner. When they finish with you, they will be well fed. There will only be a few strapping of strappings left of you. The maggots and worms will eat off of what's left. Then they will leave the bones and will round them up and burn them, so you will be ashes under the sole of the righteous foot.

But before then all of your nakedness will show, all of Satan's old cronies that sacrifice my Father's sons and daughters to Baal. Old Satan, Chief Butcher, Sun of Hannon, you use cannibalism, witchcraft, sorcery and roots on these weak minded people, taking their minds, soul and dignity. You provide money, take their land, take their cities, take their main street and tried to take the court house to find out that it belongs to the citizens of Greensboro. You take our schools, you take our children, some you turn into prostitutes, some you turn into crack heads and some you will take to hell with you. You inquired an exquisite taste of human flesh.

Satan will give you all that you want in hell. He will let you eat one of your right arms off and if you are still a little lunchy, he says he will let you eat your left one off. If you still have a little hunger pain left, to get your panties in a bunch or underwear all cross ways, both of your arms will grow back quickly. Satan is going to have a line and one big greasy demon with a big greasy hand will snatch one of you out of the crowd, strip you naked, throw you in a cave and get in the cave with you and seal it up and will take the long finger nails and strike you on your one of your butt cheeks and snatch a plug out of it and eat it in your face. He is going to snatch a big plug out of the other but cheek and eat half and give you the rest. So don't go crazy on me now because your but cheek will grow right back.

God says that he is going to stop you from lying in his name, saying, "I Dream, I Dream." He says if you have your dream, tell your dream. If you have my truth, preach my truth. He says in vain you worship him when you teach the commandments of man as doctrine. Mark 7

"You changed my time, my laws and my commandments. You say that you are doing like my Fore Fathers. But you are just like Pharisees. You travel land and sea just to convert one sinner and you turn around and make him more of a devil in hell than you are. God's holy days calendar starts his day from evening to evening. The Roman calendar starts your day one minute after midnight. God's holy calendar starts New Year in the spring of the year when everything is budding out around the middle of April.

You start your New Year dead in the heart of winter, January the first. Jeroboam changed the seventh day to the eight day, the seventh month to the eighth month. You changed the first resurrection to the rapture which is not in the Bible. The rapture only means the caught up. You used the first resurrection of scripture trying to prove the rapture. But Revelation twelve tears the rapture theory up because the church is going to be on earth because the woman which is the church escapes Satan. Satan is mad with the woman because he spit out of flood after the woman. He tried to drown her but the earth helped the woman and sucked up the flood that Satan spit out for her and Christ gave the woman the church two wings of an eagle so she might fly into the wilderness where he will have a place prepared for her, for a time, time and a half of a time, which is three and a half years. You will find out that place is Petra, where Christ will teach only his saints and the Jews will escape from Jerusalem for the three and half years while the Great Tribulation is going on, getting his saints and the Jews ready to rule with him for eleven hundred year, to judge the world and the angels. I Cor. 6:

Jeroboam changed the seventh month, with the Feast of Tabernacles or Booths to the eighth month, which is Halloween, when the wicked dead are going to be raised back into the flesh so God can change man's spirit to flesh, so Christ can burn the spirit, soul and body up. This is the third resurrection. The first resurrection is when all of the saints that died in Christ will be resurrected. The ones that will be alive with God's Holy Spirit in them will be caught up in the air with the dead and meet Christ in the air. Christ will take us and we will be changed into God beings. Christ will take us up to God the Father in the Holy of Holies where he went over two thousand year ago and will sprinkle his blood in the Holy of Holies for all man sins. And God the Father will anoint us and give us our rewards, our position that we will hold for eternity, according to our works. Matt 16:27

We will return in our glorified body with Christ and all of his holy angels and army, the same day. You say how can you do that all in one day? Christ did it over two thousand years ago. Christ told Mary Magdalene not to cling to him because he had not been to his Father yet. He said to go and tell my disciples to meet him in Jerusalem that same evening, so he did.

Christ and all of his Saints and his Army will make a sweep over Petra then his feet will strike Mt. Olive and will split it into east to west, north and south and he will go to war. Then Christ will be ruling over the earth for eleven hundreds years. Then God the Father will come. He will bring New Jerusalem after he purifies the earth. He will purify the earth with fire this time instead of water. He says then he will burn up everything that Satan has touched. Satan and all of the evil demons will be burned up. Satan will leave a skunky smell in the earth. God the Father says he will burn that up too. He then will hang New Jerusalem over old Jerusalem. New Jerusalem will be fifteen hundred miles square each way. Then God the Father and God the Son will rule the whole universe from earth. Don't need the Sun because New Jerusalem will light up the entire earth. I could go on and on but I will share a few verses.

II Peter 3
John 17
I Cor. 15
Rev 11:15
Zech. 14
Romans 8
Rev. 19
Rev. 20
Dan. 2:44
Dan. 7
Dan. 8
Isaiah 26
Isaiah 16
Dan.12

This is for the worldly preachers that skip over Revelations 20. Revelations 20 has three resurrections. I will only touch a little of Revelations 20. "And I saw an angel come down from heaven, having the key of the bottomless pit and a great chain in his hand. he laid hold on the dragon, that old serpent, which is the Devil, and Satan, and bound him a thousand years, And cast him into the bottomless pit, and shut him up, and set a seal upon him, that he should deceive the nations no more, till the thousand years should be fulfilled: and after that he must be loosed a little season. And I saw thrones, and they sat upon them, and judgment was given unto them: **[This is the first fruits.]** and I saw the souls of them that were beheaded for the witness of Jesus, and for the word of God, and which had not worshipped the beast, neither his image, neither had received his mark upon their foreheads, or in their hands; and they lived and reigned with Christ a thousand years. But the rest of the dead lived not again until the thousand years were finished. **This is the first resurrection.** Blessed and holy is he that hath part in the first resurrection: on such the second death hath no power **[Meaning they can't die anymore]**, but they shall be priests of God and of Christ, and shall reign with him a thousand years." Rev 20:1-6

I John 2:4 says that he that says I know him and keeps not his commandment is a liar and the truth is not in him.

Christ says that any man that does not keep my commandments shall be called the least in the kingdom of heaven. Matt. 5:17-20

Gat 1:1-8 says if an angel from heaven comes down preaching another gospel than what we preach, he will have a double curse on him. So people cannot change anything. II Peter 1:19-20

Christ was walking through the fields with his disciples on the Sabbath. They were hungry and he plucked some grain and ate it. The Pharisees saw them and wanted to stone them and Christ told them he was the Lord of the Sabbath. He made the Sabbath; he rested on it, and put his holy name in it so he will not tire. He was just setting an example for us to follow. So the Sabbath is not only the Jews day. He set it aside so man could get his rest and the animals are refreshed for the next seven days. But you know more than Christ because you want to make your own day. Christ said he does not put any trust in any man. He called Jacob a worm. He says that the whole heaven and universe is not pure in his site. In 325 AD, Constantine and the counselors of Laodicea met and decided you must not Judaize by resting on the Sabbath. But you must work on that day and keep the day of the sun, Sunday, and worship the Sun God. The Egyptians Sun God was named "On". The Caananite sun god was named "Baal". So Constantine repented on the death bed three days before he died. I don't think you can repent that quickly because God reproduced himself through man.

The great GOD cannot create perfect righteous character by fiat. So Constantine was just like a King, he ordered all religions to come together at the Church of the Nativity because they were all at war against one another. He brought Catholicism, Judaism, Pagan, and Christianity. He took the pagan days and put Christian names on them. The Pagans were happy, the Christians were happy and they were one big happy family. They say that they have a Western Religion but wanted to keep the Eastern traditions. They are still kissing the calf that was set up in Dan and one in Samaria (Northern Israel). They worship Idols and changed Christ's birthday. When Christ was born in Bethlehem, the sheep and the shepherds were in the field and the Holy Angel came singing. They told the shepherds that he was being born in Bethlehem. The shepherds left the sheep and went to Bethlehem to worship the king. Anyone that knows anything about Jewish history or custom knows that they bring their sheep, cattle and goats in no later than September or the first of October to put the sheep in the barn to be ready to sham them for the winter. So Christ could not have been born in December. Constantine took a pagan day and put a Christian name on it and called it Christmas. That is why you call them bulbs on a Christmas tree, Nimrod bulbs. When they killed Nimrod, his mother wife Queen Semiramis wanted his power. She told everybody that Nimrod came back over night as a Christmas Tree. She had all of the world power because she had fornicated with all of the Kings of the earth. She and two more Black Queens, even the Roman Empire was afraid of them. They built the city of Nineveh with a sixty mile long wall. Nimrod was the first Chinese King. They called him bright eyes because he was demon possessed. We would call him a red eye roast because he was blue black just like the Nile River. Josephus says Jesus Christ was a Black Caananite Jew who spoke Hebrew, Aramaic, was four feet nine inches tall, and had kinky hair. The Hebrew language is the old Caananite language. Christ had a brother in Act 13:1 called Simon the Caananite called "Nigger" "Niiger" "Niger". He was named after the Nile River. Christ had five brother and three sisters.

Noah was born snow white. He had bright eyes and illuminated the room that he was in, but he was righteous. Christ says that he was born light that because of the sins of the angels. Noah's father saw his son and became afraid of him because he was snow white. He ran half way around the world and found Enoch. Enoch told Noah's father not to be afraid because that was God's doing. Enoch said that God the Father showed them his new body and his old body was melting, was turning into spiritual flesh and bone, just like the same body that Jesus Christ was resurrected in. Enoch was translated to heaven without seeing death.

But God told Enoch that he could not stay in heaven because he had to go back to earth so that all of the fresh fruit could come in at the same time. So the rapture theory does not hold up because half of the Laodiceans will take the mark of the beast and they will be resurrected in the third resurrection. Just be burned up. And one half will lose their head. They will be in the first resurrection. That will be the end of the tribulation. Hebrew 11 tells you the same, that all the saints traveled through deserts and caves looking for a city that was not made with hands. They all died in faith not receiving the promise. We, the firstfruits, have something much better for us. They cannot enter the kingdom apart from us alive when Christ returns. The first fruits are going in at the same time. Rev 6.

So if you would like know what Nimrod and Queen Semiramis were, ask any Polish or Catholic person and they will tell you proudly because they worship the Black Madonna. If you would like to know a little something about the Christmas Tree, Jeremiah 10 will tell you. Valentine's Day is baby Nimrod playing cupid. Easter is the Great Madonna that fell down from Zeus. Act 19 when that old silversmith wanted to kill Paul he made the statue of the Great Madonna. The silversmith says that this old Paul has turned this world upside down saying that the Great Madonna is not a Goddess but the whole world knows that the Great Statue fell down from Zeus and the whole world worship the Great Madonna. The Great Madonna was a Roman Pagan Goddess with twenty one breasts.

Jeremiah 44 chapter says that the Great Madonna calls herself the Queen of heaven. Jeremiah 7 says you bake hot cross buns and bake cakes for the Queen of Heaven. You dress up real pretty on a Sunday and have to have something new on for the Queen of Heaven. Ezekiel 8 says look at the people that have this wood to make the little gods out of gold and silver. They called the statue "my mother" and the rock "my father". Just like evolution. Our ideas about heaven and hell were made popular by Plato and the book Dante's Inferno. Evolution says that rain beat on a rock for millions of years and the pieces of rock broke off and turned into one single cell, but they don't know their science. One single cell has factories, cities and pieces of the universe in it. To put it simply, it is just like an automobile. You can turn that starter all you would like but, if all of the parts are not working simultaneously, it will not start. So this is with a single cell, everything had to work at the same time. They will not split and multiply, they will die.

Scientists have found in the rainforest dinosaur tracks, human being tracks walking along side of them. This is the missing links that scientists are in search of. From the first man and Adam is millions of years is the missing link. The Big Bang Theory says that the universe goes back to one little dot and everything comes from that one little dot that spread out. Every planet turns around on its axis in perfect alignment. That just sort of happened? You can set your watch by it. If the planets were a few yards too close to the sun, they would burn up. If they were a few yards back from the sun they would freeze. So you are trying to tell me that a whirlwind went through a junk yard and built a plane, put two or three hundred people on it and started flying, that it just sort of happened? You cannot get anything from nothingness. You have to have a mass before you can have nothingness. The earth was smaller than it is today. It had two atmospheres, the canopy was thicker and that is why the dinosaurs could breathe more easily because the canopy was thick. People think that we are getting smarter but in all actually we are getting dumber. When babies were born in those days, they could get plenty air because they had seven thousand times more brain cells than now and could receive more oxygen. But half of the baby brain cells die before they leave the womb because the canopy is thinner and they can't get enough oxygen.

Scientists have discovered whales with half of a fish sticking out of their mouth. They also found dinosaurs bones with little dinosaurs half way sticking out of their mouth. Something happened over the entire universe and froze everything in time. When Satan tried to take over God's throne they fought over the whole universe. This is where the depiction of star wars originated from. That is why the entire universe is in decay now.

There is nothing that has been renewed except the earth. This is why Man was created, to renew the entire universe. This is why Rom. 8 says that "the entire creation is awaiting on the redemption of the sons of God.", changing man into God beings so God the Father can be all over the universe in human form to beautify the entire universe like the earth was done and will be done.

In Ezekiel 8, Ezekiel is taken in the spirit to Jerusalem. He is taken outside the gate and shown great abominations that Israel was doing. The worst was a crowd of people facing the east. Look, they are worshiping something towards the east. It couldn't be God's throne because it is in the far, far side of the north. Because Satan said that he was going to take over God's throne and sat on it in the far, far side of the North. (Isaiah 14) So these people facing the east were worshiping the sun in the east. That was what Satan was called, the "Day Star", so when you hold your Easter sunrise service, read your congregation Ezekiel 8.

Cush was a genius. He invented navigation, the arts and ship building. He created numbers, agriculture, astronomy and chess. Nimrod was so wicked that he killed his own father Cush and married his own mother Queen Semiramis. Shem heard about it and he chased Nimrod to Egypt. I wonder why Ham did not chase Nimrod to Egypt because it was his son whom Nimrod killed. Josephus said that when Ham died, Shem and Ham became one nation. Nimrod escaped Shem and went to Rome and set up a statue in the Vatican Square and called himself "A PETER" and told the Pope that he was going to transfer the church to the Pope. It is true today the Catholic is the father all Churches. So Shem killed Nimrod and cut him up in twelve pieces and sent them to the twelve tribes of Israel. So when the twelve tribes came back together, they pieced Nimrod back together to see if all of the twelve tribes had made it. All of Nimrod was there except two little pieces and they still look for those two little pieces today. You have your little children Easter Eggs hunting today. Actually you are looking for Nimrod's two little pieces that are missing, what they say that the dog got. What do eggs have to do with Christ's resurrection? A bunny rabbit is unclean just like a pig. They poured swine blood on God's altar (throne) and made it unholy. They were worshiping fertility gods. They worshipped everything that reproduces fast. Like a fish, rabbit, a woman's womb. Even your church windows are in the shape of a woman's womb, the steeple a symbol of an uncircumcised penis, like the Washington monument where the earthquake hit. God got tired of an uncircumcised penis sticking up in his face.

I do not know how long after the flood but the babies of Israel in Lower Egypt (Alexandria) started being born like Noah, pure white. I am not sure how holy they were like Noah, but the Egyptians said that they were defending their god. They ran them out of Lower Egypt to Israel. They held their annual feast of tabernacles with about six million Israelites. They had an old custom which was to take a pail and turn it upside down and they would sacrifice a dove, or pigeon and they would cry out "unclean" "unclean". They were speaking of Ezekiel16. In Leviticus 13, they ran them out of Jerusalem and they went to Libya. They left there and went to North West Africa. This is when the history ended for some people. Finally, Israel received Abraham's blessing. It took them 2520 years because God would conquer nations for them. They would take the women and their Gods and worship idols. GOD will take his hand off of them and the same nation would re-conquer them and they would run and hide in caves and rocks and holes. They would slip out at night and kill animals and take them back in the caves to skin them and get ready to cook them.

But they decided not to make a fire because the enemy would see their smoke. This is where the rare steak comes from. Some people like to eat rare steak. When Jacob was dying he told Joseph the son to bring his two sons so he could pass on the birthright to them. Rueben was the oldest and should have had the birthright, the double portion of Abraham blessing. But he was caught in the bed with his father's wife (concubine) so he lost his birth right like Esau, which is modern day Turkey. So Joseph brought his two sons Ephraim and Manasseh. He put the oldest one on the right side and the youngest one on his left side. But Jacob crossed his hands and put his right hand on the youngest one Ephraim and the left one on Manasseh who was the oldest. Joseph said, "not so my father" and Joseph put his father's hand on the right one Manasseh. Jacob said the he knew his son. The oldest one is going to be one great nation Manasseh. But the youngest one Ephraim will a company of nations.

You can search history and you can only find two nations that fit. They had an old saying that the sun never set on the British Empire. It did not because Great Britain had conquered one third but almost one half of the known world. The sun has gone down now on them and then Manasseh migrated from Great Britain to the United States and became thirteen Colonies. They stayed small until they made that Louisiana Purchase from the French, who are Reuben's descendants that should have gotten Abraham double portion.

Between the U.S. and Great Britain, they owned two thirds of the known world and all the sea gates, Panama Canal, Sunil Canal, etc. Now they have lost all of the canals and the rest of the gates. They only have Louisiana gates. The U.S. is getting ready to isolate itself. They say they are going to migrate to Louisiana like they have taken over Atlanta. They say the Louisiana is the only gate they now have.

This will not do the U.S. any good because God the Father and God the Son is going to give Israel a spanking that they will not forget. He says he will not pass by Israel anymore. God the Father and God the Son had the pot filled and cocked ready to pour out onto the U.S. and Great Britain, part of Canada, Australia and Armenia. In London, England there will not be a brick left on top of another. One third will die by pestilence, diseases, drugs, legal and illegal. God the Father will take the dread out of the animals that he put into them so man could rule the earth, so your own pet will turn on you. The second one third is going to die in nuclear war. All sinners will die of that one third because God the Father will stop all witchcraft, roots, unbalanced scale, adultery, robbing the poor, selling rotten meat and molding bread. All sinners will die so he can have mercy on them. God the Father has promised Israel that all would be saved. They are enemies of the Gospel but they are beloved for the Father's sake. GOD will scatter them all over the world as you would scatter wheat but not a grain will hit the ground.

People talk about Ezekiel 37 and do not know what it really means. When you talk about those dry bones "Son of Man, will these bone live"? Those bones were really dry. The wind started blowing and the bones started rallying and started coming together sinew came upon the bones, skin covered the bone and all of those dry bones stood on their feet and it was a great army. It was the whole house of Israel. So, all of Israel will be saved. Some will be saved in the first resurrection and some in the second resurrection, along with everyone else that ever lived. They will know God and will be resurrected in the second resurrection, all except the incredibly wicked. They will be resurrected in the third resurrection back into their fleshly bodies, just to change their spirit to matter, which is flesh, just to be burned up in spirit and body.

I don't know what kind of God you all serve but you should try mine. You think that God is going to condemn you to hell for eternity for not knowing or hearing his name. Everybody that ever lived is going to be resurrected and live a hundred years to be taught by God and his saints. He says that he will give his first-fruits in the first resurrection the privilege of raising their own parents from the dead and making them princes and princesses for a hundred years in the flesh and then be changed into a God being.

Psalms 45 says "Instead of your father being your father you will be his father." Everyone's resurrected body will not become more than twenty nine years old. But they will live a hundred years. A child will live a hundred years and then be changed into a God being.

An old man who lives to be a hundred years old in a twenty nine old body who won't repent will die in his sins and be resurrected in the third resurrection. God the Father will give Israel a threshing machine that will cut down all mountain to make it level so for people to live because billions and billions of people will have space to live. Deserts will blossom like a rose, with box trees and rivers will run through. GOD will hit the ocean and it will break up in rivers and streams making room for man. Every yard of ocean will have gold on it. This is where God will get the gold to pave the streets over in Jerusalem.

Take the small nation of Israel. It will turn from a desert into an oasis. Israel is now furnishing all of the fruits and vegetables for Europe and U.S. They have irrigation systems where the water doesn't touch the ground but goes straight to the roots. Now they have struck oil and they will be the top producers.

The last one-third of Israel will go into captivity and he will pull out a sword behind them and it will be five months that Israel will want to die and will be unable to die. Death is going to flee from them. Only one-eight will survive. They will bring them over on horses and mules to Jerusalem where we will be because all of the electricity will be out. Mostly it will be the children and great grandchildren. We will clean them up and one half of Judea will go into captivity. Matt. 24

If you are on a house top, do not come down. If you are in the field, do not come back to get your coat, and hope that your wife will not be pregnant in them days, or be in the winter, or on the Sabbath. Because the beast power and the false prophet will rape the Jewish women, cut them open who are with child but most of that one half of Israel will escape to a place called Petra sixty miles from Jordan. Petra is where Christ will be, with the church. Revelations 12 says that Christ has a place prepared for her for a time, and time, and a half of time.

Petra is where the Jews first meet Christ and the church will be taught along with the Jews when the tribulation is going on for three and a half years, getting us ready to rule with Christ for eleven hundred years. Christ will bring Judea and Israel back together and make them one nation again.

To Benny Hinn and Reinhard Bonnke

TO BENNY HINN
AND REINHARD BONNKE

Pastor Benny, I was listening to one of your programs when you said you was on a bus with an old lady going to a meeting and arthritis had her twisted up like a pretzel and she got healed in one of your meetings. You could see her unraveling because her foot was turning back straight and she was healed up perfectly except her little pinky. She asked after she was healed if they could heal the crook in her finger and they said no because when you look at your little finger you will know that GOD healed you.

The same thing happened to me when I had that first love with Christ Jesus. My whole hand was cut off and there was nothing holding it except the skin and I did not know what to do. The Holy Spirit told me to stick my hand inside my shirt and I was healed instantly. I had a little crook in my finger and I asked the Lord the same thing that little lady did and he told me the same thing. Then God started revealing his glory to me. I did not go to heaven but he brought heaven to me and he showed me everything that will happen in heaven. He showed me all the glory that will be coming in the second coming. He showed me that you do not have time to ask for something it happens instantaneous. He showed me that if you can speak in the old Hebrew language in certain dialect you can speak anything into being like he spoke and the foundation of the earth was uncovered the face of the earth. I stayed with that first love for seven years, studied night and day. God fixed it so I could study on my jobs for three or four days out of a week and I got paid for it. I have been studying for thirty-two years, but enough about me.

I want to speak about you Pastor Benn. You also stated where Elijah came into your room and he just looked at you and did not say a thing. But Pastor Benn he was passing his mantle to you because the mantle had not went anywhere because Elisha died with the mantle still on him but Gehazi became greedy and his entire family was struck with leprosy. So in the II King13:21 as men were burying a dead man, they ran upon raiders, so they hid the dead body in Elisha's tomb and the dead body touched Elisha's bones and the dead man's body came back to life. So the mantle had not departed from Elisha.

Christ said so himself when they asked when Elijah shall come and restore all things. Christ said Matt 11:14 "If you are willing to receive it he is John the Baptist." Elijah has already come and shall come. So John the Baptist came in the spirit of Elijah. John the Baptist died in prison so the mantle is still on earth. So Elijah's mantle has been passed to you. Pastor Benny Hinn and Reinhard Bonnke are the two witnesses in Rev.11 and II Cor. 4:3-4.

Pastor Benny, please study Revelations 11 and decide for yourself.

Tower of Babel

TOWER OF BABEL

When Nimrod was building the Tower of Babel, he wasn't only trying to build a tall building. He knew where the portal was that Christ used for his angel to transport from heaven to earth. So when Christ came down and saw that Nimrod was building the tower, Christ came down and confused their language so everyone spoke a different language. Satan knew were the portal was and he bombarded the weakest ones and fooled his general and went through the portal and his general had to change into a human body and he can't change back. He is stuck in a human body, guarding Satan's son.

This general has high blood pressure and all types of diseases. He is suffering and has to die in the body of a human because he can't change back. Christ's angel volunteered to be changed into human body to watch Satan's general and his son. He calculated now that his son is about thirty years old.

Epilogue

The sons of Adam spread across the face of the earth. Cain, the first child of the first couple, grew up to be a murderer. Other descendants, carrying within them the disease of sin, fared no better. The Lord, therefore, destroyed man's civilization in a deluge of water, saving from its destruction one family only.

One of the surviving sons of that small family turned out to be no better than those who had lived before the flood. Only a brief time passed before the face of the earth was once more populated by the mutated species called fallen man.

During those times, the door between the heavens and earth opened on only the rarest occasions.

But there did come a most memorable day when the Lord, in the company with Gabriel and Michael, stood at the passageway between the two realms and commanded the door to open. The Lord stepped upon the door's threshold, while Michael and Gabriel waited, and observed.

"A place even farther east than the land of Babylon.", said Michael, looking out upon the scene that lay before them.

"There", replied Gabriel, as he pointed toward a man intently involved in the skinning of pigs.

"That is the one to whom the Lord will speak this day. It appears his occupation is raising live-stock. I see cows, sheep, goats, and pigs."

"What purpose lies behind the Lord's desire to speak to this unwashed Gentile?", wondered both archangels.

"Look! One of the man's servants has called him to the noon meal. It seems the man's favorite meat is pork."

"Why would the Lord wish to speak to an uncircumcised heathen?"

At that moment the Lord called out the man.

"ABRAM!" (Abraham)

Appendixes

VATICAN

<u>SAINT PETER'S BASILICA</u> <u>THE VATICAN MUSEUMS &</u> <u>GALLERIES - THE TREASURE</u> <u>OF SAINT PETER - THE</u> <u>FIRST POPE</u> - (FROM 64 AD TO 1453 AD ALL OF THE POPES WERE BLACK HEBREW ISRAELITES)

THIS STATUE WAS COMPLETED IN THE 11TH CENTURY.

81

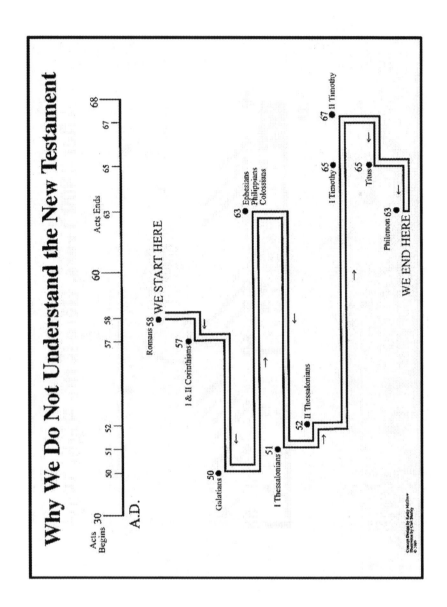

Why We Do Not Understand the New Testament

After 1800 Years, Here is the Right Way

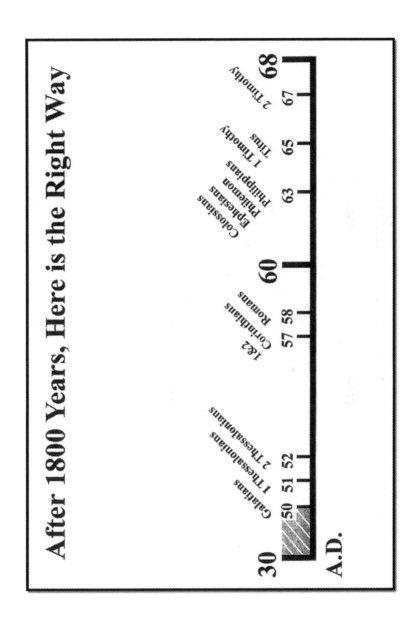

A.D.

30 50 51 52 57 58 60 63 65 67 68

Galatians
1 Thessalonians
2 Thessalonians

1&2 Corinthians
Romans

Colossians
Ephesians
Philemon
Philippians

1 Timothy
Titus

2 Timothy

Twelve Tribes of Israel

Tribes	Modern Nations
GAD	Switzerland
Ruben	France
Semi on and Levi	Scattered in Israel
Judah	Scattered
Zebulon	Holland
Issachar	Finland
DAN	Denmark and Ireland
Asher	Belgium and Luxemburg
Naphtali	Sweden
Ephraim	Britain
Manasseh	United States
Benjamin	Norway
Salvation is merely the completing of creation	Spiritual creation is still in process

*Autumn of 27 A.D. to the Passover in 31 A.D.
Christ Teaching Dan9:27

The Annual Feast Days of God

Roman Year	First Day of Sacred Year	*Passover	Days of Unleavened Bread	**Pentecost	Feast of Trumpets	Day of Atonement	Feast of Tabernacles	The Last Great Day
	Nisan (or Abib) 1	Nisan 14	Nisan 15-21	Sivan	Tishri 1	Tishri 10	Tishri 15-21	Tishri 22
2006	March-30	April-12	April 13-19	June-4	September-23	October-2	October 7-13	October-14
2007	March-20	April-2	April 3-9	May-27	September-13	September-22	Sept. 27-Oct. 3	October-4
2008	April-6	April-19	April 20-26	June-8	September-30	October-9	October 14-20	October-21
2009	March-26	April-8	April 9-15	May-31	September-19	September-28	October 3-9	October-10
2010	March-16	March-29	Mar. 30-Apr. 5	May-23	September-9	September-18	September 23-29	September-30
2011	April-5	April-18	April 19-25	June-12	September-29	October-8	October 13-19	October-20
2012	March-24	April-6	April 7-13	May-27	September-17	September-26	October 1-7	October-8
2013	March-12	March-25	Mar. 26-Apr.1	May-19	September-5	September-14	September 19-25	September-26

* Observed the pevious evening after sunset. Fpr example, in 2006 the Passover would be observed the evening of April 11.

** Pentecost (a Greek word signifying "fiftieth") is counted from the day on whih the wave sheaf was offered during the Days of Unleavened Bread. It is always on a Sunday during Sivan, the third month.

IMAGE 5:

THE FIRST
INHABITANTS
OF BRITAIN
WERE BLACK
HEBREW
ISRAELITES.
FAMILY CREST
FOR BRITAIN.

(Black Hebrew Israelite) (Jew) in Britain First inhabitants

Plate I. Family crest from Britain with pronounced Africoid features. "The first inhabitants of Britain and most especially those of the southern parts, were contemporaries of... those exactly like the Negro." MacRitchie photo from the Prutton collection.

ON HIS LAP

JESUS CHRIST

JESUS CHRIST SITTING AMONG THE DOCTORS

MARY AND JESUS CHRIST

JESUS CHRIST AND THE 12